AN UNOFFICIAL ACTIVITY BOOK

VOCABULARY

FOR

MINECRAFTERS

ACTIVITIES TO HELP KIDS BOOST
READING AND LANGUAGE SKILLS

Grades 3-4

Sky Pony Press
New York, New York

Copyright © 2022 by Hollan Publishing, Inc.

Minecraft® is a registered trademark of Notch Development AB.

The Minecraft game is copyright © Mojang AB.

Sky Pony Press books may be purchased in bulk at special discounts for sales promotion, corporate gifts, fund-raising, or educational purposes. Special editions can also be created to specifications. For details, contact the Special Sales Department, Sky Pony Press, 307 West 36th Street, 11th Floor, New York, NY 10018 or info@skyhorsepublishing.com.

Sky Pony® is a registered trademark of Skyhorse Publishing, Inc.®, a Delaware corporation.

Visit our website at www.skyhorsepublishing.com.

10 9 8 7 6 5 4 3 2 1

Library of Congress Cataloging-in-Publication Data is available on file.

Cover and interior illustration by Grace Sandford

Book design by Noora Cox

Print ISBN: 978-1-5107-7110-9

Printed in China

A NOTE TO PARENTS

Build their vocabulary, one fun activity at a time!

When you want to reinforce classroom skills at home, it's crucial to have kid-friendly learning materials. This *Vocabulary for Minecrafters* workbook transforms language development into an irresistible adventure complete with diamond swords, zombies, skeletons, and ghasts.

Vocabulary for Minecrafters is also fully aligned with National Common Core Standards for 3rd and 4th grade English Language Arts (ELA). Encourage your child to progress at his or her own pace. Learning is best when students are challenged, but not frustrated. What's most important is that your Minecrafter is engaged in his or her own learning.

With more than 50 gamer-friendly practice pages, puzzles, and Minecraft-themed illustrations, your child will be eager to dive in and level up their reading and vocabulary skills.

Happy adventuring!

SHADES OF MEANING

Write the adjectives in the chart to add power to the word's meaning.

| ~~tiny~~ | awful | terrified | afraid | horrendous |
| great | ~~microscopic~~ | jog | excellent | run |

small	tiny	microscopic
good		
worried		
bad		
walk		

Use one of the words in the word box to describe what's happening in the picture:

_____

_____

THE POWER OF PREFIXES

Add the correct prefix to the space provided to change the meaning of the root word.

dis-	un-

1. The location of the stronghold was _____known.

2. Steve was _____armed when he entered the Nether.

3. The potion of Invisibility made her _____appear.

4. The explosive green mob really _____likes cats.

5. I feel _____safe when I see a piglin and I'm not wearing gold armor.

6. Milk can _____do the effects of certain potions.

DESCRIBING WORDS

Use an adverb from the box to finish the sentence.

blindly	loudly	quickly
noticeably	incredibly	increasingly

1. The ghast screeches _____ .

2. Potion of Swiftness makes me move _____ .

3. The spotted spawn egg is _____ different from the others.

4. She grew _____ nervous as the zombies got closer.

5. The dolphins are _____ skilled at finding treasure.

6. Without torches to help him, he fumbled _____ through the dark cave.

SYNONYMS

Synonyms are words that mean almost the same thing.
Finish the sentence with a synonym for the word provided.

1. That little shulker is surprisingly _____ .
   (fearsome)

2. Golden apples can be very _____ .
   (valuable)

3. It was a _____ move to set that zombie trap.
   (smart)

4. It took me many _____ to destroy the
   Ender dragon.   *(attempts)*

5. A diamond sword is extremely _____ .
   (strong)

Write three synonyms below describing
how you feel when you get good loot.

_____

_____

_____

RELATIVE PRONOUNS

Fill in the blank with a relative pronoun from the word box.

Who	Whose	Which

1. **QUESTION:** _____ swamp hut is that?

   ANSWER: It belongs to a witch.

2. **QUESTION:** _____ of your swords will you use?

   ANSWER: I will use my gold sword.

3. **QUESTION:** _____ gave you that rabbit's foot?

   ANSWER: A cleric gave it to me.

4. **QUESTION:** _____ is guarding the village?

   ANSWER: The iron golem is guarding it.

5. **QUESTION:** _____ house do you want to meet at?

   ANSWER: Let's meet at your house.

Now write your own question about Minecraft using a relative pronoun. Then write the answer.

QUESTION: _____

ANSWER: _____

SIGHT WORD CROSSWORD

Sight words are words that appear many times in the books you read. Learn them and reading will be easier! Read the clues and write the sight word in the puzzle.

ACROSS

3 an idea

5 opposite of dark

6 What you use to see.

9 opposite of always

DOWN

1 opposite of finish

2 a tale

4 opposite of low

7 Each and _____ one of us plays Minecraft.

8 opposite of give away

MATH WORD SCRAMBLE

Unscramble the math words below. Use the words in the word box to help you.

area	polygon	factor
perimeter	plot	multiple
unit	equivalent	quotient

1. raae _____

2. timerpeer _____

3. tuni _____

4. golypon _____

5. avlueiquent _____

6. tlop _____

7. roaftc _____

8. pieltlum _____

9. toenutiq _____

NOUNS, ADJECTIVES, VERBS, AND ADVERBS

Underline the **nouns** in the sentence below.

1. Steve caught a very large fish.

Circle the **adjectives** in the sentence below.

2. Steve was excited when he saw the red fish on his line.

Draw a box around the **verbs** in the sentence below.

3. Steve pulled on the rod and reeled in the fish.

Put a checkmark above the **adverbs** in the sentence below.

4. The fish flapped noisily as Steve pulled quickly on the rod.

Write your own sentences about the picture using a **noun**, an **adjective**, a **verb**, and an **adverb**.

5. _____

6. _____

IRREGULAR PLURAL NOUNS

Match each noun with its irregular plural form.

1. tooth   women

2. woman   shelves

3. fish   children

4. person   mice

5. foot   teeth

6. child   fishes

7. mouse   people

8. shelf   feet

PLURAL NOUNS

Add **-s** or **-es** to make each noun plural.

SINGULAR	PLURAL
box	
computer	
glass	
book	
class	
potato	
school	

REGULAR VERB TENSES

A **tense** tells the time when something happened. Fill in the chart with the correct tense of these regular verbs. The first one is done for you.

BASE FORM	PAST	PRESENT	FUTURE
play	played	plays	will play
call		calls	
walk	walked		
clean			will clean
climb		climbs	
look	looked		

IRREGULAR PAST TENSE VERBS

Use the words from the box to write the past tense of the verb in the sentence.

1. Alex _____ dinner.
   (eat)

2. Steve _____ late.
   (sleep)

3. He _____ to school yesterday.
   (go)

4. She _____ on the plane to see her grandma.
   (fly)

5. The teacher _____ to the class.
   (speak)

6. The ghast _____ up tall.
   (stand)

7. I _____ an essay on my summer vacation.
   (write)

8. She _____ the book for homework.
   (read)

COMPARING WORDS

Fill in the chart to make a **comparative** or **superlative** adjective. The first one is done for you.

ADJECTIVE	COMPARATIVE	SUPERLATIVE
tall	taller	tallest
loud		loudest
good	better	
smart		smartest
cold	colder	
bright	brighter	
soft		softest
sweet		

COMPARATIVE AND SUPERLATIVE ADJECTIVES

Choose the **comparative** or **superlative** adjectives on page 14 to complete the sentences.

1. The sun is _____ in the summer than in the winter.   *(bright)*

2. The Enderman is _____ than the zombie.   *(tall)*

3. Alex is the _____ person I know.   *(smart)*

4. This pillow is the _____ one.   *(soft)*

5. Minecraft cookies are _____ than mushroom stew.   *(sweet)*

6. The Snowy Tundra is the _____ biome I've visited.   *(cold)*

7. This Minecraft update is _____ than the last one.   *(good)*

8. The wither's cry was the _____ thing I have ever heard.   *(loud)*

LANGUAGE ARTS WORD SCRAMBLE

Unscramble the language arts words below. Use the words in the word box to help you.

adverb	character	conflict	dialogue
	fact	opinion	phrase

1. iponnio _____

2. bverad _____

3. acrhretca _____

4. tfac _____

5. tocifcnl _____

6. erhaps _____

7. gdaoleiu _____

SCIENCE
WORD SCRAMBLE

Unscramble the science words below. Use the words in the word box to help you.

carnivore	community	erosion	volcano
herbivore		microscope	prey

1. vroheerbi _____

2. reyp _____

3. snoorie _____

4. evrciaron _____

5. pemisrocco _____

6. mnciuymot _____

7. ocvoaln _____

SINGULAR POSSESSIVE

Rewrite each phrase to show possession. The first one is done for you.

1. The potion of the witch

   <u>The witch's potion</u>

2. The saddle of the horse

   _____

3. The arm of the zombie

   _____

4. The sword of Alex

   _____

5. The egg of the chicken

   _____

6. The minecart of the player

   _____

7. The pickaxe of Steve

   _____

PLURAL POSSESSIVE

Fill in the chart with the correct form of the word. The first one is done for you.

SINGULAR NOUN	PLURAL NOUN	PLURAL POSSESSIVE NOUN
ghast	ghasts	ghasts'
player		
	zombies	
		creepers'
dragon		
	villagers	
librarian		
		witches'
	griefers	

SIGHT WORD SEARCH

Sight words are words that appear many times in the books you read. Learn them and reading will be easier! Find the words in the word search puzzle.

```
F  A  M  I  L  Y  D  M  N
R  T  D  V  R  P  O  A  T
C  U  T  Q  D  U  G  O  J
W  O  W  R  N  E  G  R  Y
M  H  U  T  B  E  E  O  J
Z  T  A  N  T  H  U  B  M
K  I  Y  H  T  N  N  Z  T
N  W  E  A  G  R  J  B  M
J  R  F  P  K  M  Y  J  P
```

began	without
father	family
mountain	young
together	country

SIGHT WORD CROSSWORD

Sight words are words that appear many times in the books you read. Learn them and reading will be easier! Read the clues and write the sight words in the puzzle.

ACROSS

2 Something you write on

3 Something you ask

5 The opposite of soft

6 The planet we live on

DOWN

1 What you use to buy things

2 Something you solve

4 What comes after first place

5 The opposite of low

SUPER SUFFIXES

A **suffix** is a letter or collection of letters that go at the end of a word and change the meaning of the word. Add the correct suffix to the space provided to change the meaning of the root word.

-ful	-less

1. Alex was fear_____ when she saw the zombies.

2. Steve is help_____ without his diamond armor.

3. The witch had a rainbow of

   color_____ potions.

4. The sight of the Ender dragon

   left the player speech_____ .

5. I'm good at this game, so

   I'm hope_____ I'll win.

6. Steve was getting angry at the end_____ mob attacks.

Write your own Minecraft sentence using a word with suffix -ful or -less.

_____

ANTONYMS

An **antonym** is a word that means the opposite. Match each word with its antonym.

1. quiet   below

2. above   friend

3. empty   large

4. cold   loud

5. small   full

6. enemy   asleep

7. awake   hot

Write three antonyms below for the word **sad**.

_____ _____ _____

SIGHT WORD SEARCH

Sight words are words that appear many times in the books you read. Find the words in the word search puzzle.

G	R	O	U	N	D	P	P	M
C	Y	B	Y	W	R	W	O	N
D	O	D	E	O	V	R	Z	E
D	Y	M	D	C	N	X	R	Z
G	R	U	P	I	O	U	M	B
V	C	A	N	L	S	M	D	B
T	G	G	E	A	E	Y	E	J
Q	Q	B	E	H	J	T	T	P
L	T	M	W	V	M	R	E	R

complete   ground

morning   heard

measure   become

product

IRREGULAR PAST TENSE

The **past tense** shows that something has already happened. Fill in the chart with the past tense of these irregular verbs. The first one is done for you.

BASE FORM	PAST TENSE
eat	ate
think	
throw	
sing	
hear	
go	
is	
sit	

PLURAL NOUNS

To make some nouns **plural**, you need to change the ending **-y** to **-ies**. Write the correct plural form of the word on the line. The first one is done for you.

SINGULAR   PLURAL

1. family   _____families_____

2. fly   _____

3. berry   _____

4. baby   _____

5. city   _____

6. country   _____

7. memory   _____

PREPOSITIONS

The **prepositions** in the word box show where two things are in relation to each other. Use the picture to help you fill in the blank with a preposition. The first one is done for you.

inside	beneath	behind	above
below	~~next to~~		in front of

1. Steve is sitting ___next to___ his dog.

2. The bone is _____ the dog's mouth.

3. The ground is _____ his feet.

4. He is standing _____ his house.

5. The igloo is _____ the polar bear.

6. The ghast is floating _____ Steve's head.

7. Steve is _____ the ghast.

WHAT HAPPENS WHEN

Words like *first*, *next*, and *finally* show when events take place in relation to each other. These are **temporal (or time) relationship** words. Use the time relationship words to help you put the sentences below in order from 1 to 5.

_____ Finally, Steve shut the cage with the bunny inside.

_____ Then, Steve placed a line of carrots leading to a cage.

___1___ First, Steve collected a bunch of carrots.

_____ Next, Steve placed a cage on the ground.

_____ Eventually, the bunny wandered into the cage.

FREQUENTLY CONFUSED WORDS

Homophones are words that sound the same but are spelled differently and mean different things. Write the correct homophone on the line to complete the sentence.

1. The Endermen are in _____ .
   (their, they're, there)

2. I see _____ Endermen.
   (too, two, to)

3. _____ time for me to go.
   (It's, Its)

4. It's too loud. I can't _____ you.
   (hear, here)

5. _____ going to have to make sure they don't escape.
   (Your, You're)

6. They look hungry. Should I offer them a _____ of cake?
   (piece, peace)

POSSESSIVES

The **possessive** form shows ownership.

Examples:

The player's health bar is low.
The women's team won the trophy.

Rewrite each phrase to show possession. Some are singular and some are plural. The first one is done for you.

1. **The hut of the witch**

   <u>The witch's hut</u>

2. **The cave of the spiders**

   _____

3. **The eyes of the dragon**

   _____

4. **The torches of Alex**

   _____

5. **The level of the player**

   _____

6. **The fish of the ocelot**

   _____

7. **The crafting table of Steve**

   _____

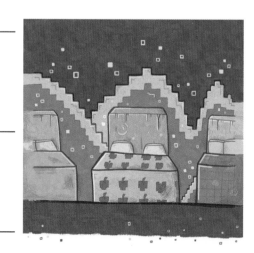

SIGHT WORD SEARCH

Sight words are words that appear many times in the books you read. Learn them and reading will be easier! Find the words in the word search puzzle.

```
E X A M P L E A I
P Y Q G Q X L M G
V D M R R W P M X
Q R L T A O I R D
P B T Y R G U Q N
M E S T H E R P J
Q I A T J B V D Q
P N L G J W X E K
T G L E M N Z N N
```

example	important
group	never
always	being
might	mile

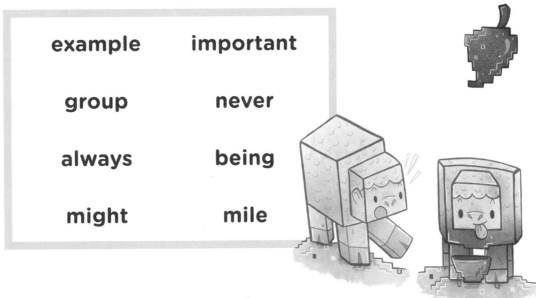

SIGHT WORD CROSSWORD

Sight words are words that appear many times in the books you read. Learn them and reading will be easier! Read the clues and write the sight words in the puzzle.

ACROSS

3 Something you listen to

4 Opposite of tall

6 Opposite of sit

7 The _____ bird catches the worm

8 What 60 minutes makes

DOWN

1 Salmon is a kind of _____

2 Animals that fly

5 Another word for command

SCIENCE WORD SCRAMBLE

Unscramble the science words below. Use the words in the word box to help you.

ecosystem	gravity	matter	solid
energy	habitat	predator	volume

1. lovmue _____

2. tthaiba _____

3. rmetat _____

4. cmeoysset _____

5. dliso _____

6. rodtrpea _____

7. vtigary _____

8. greeyn _____

OPPOSITE WORDS

An **antonym** is a word that means the opposite. Use the words in the word box to write the antonym on the line.

daytime   happy   young   dirty

neat   sunny   hard

1. easy _____

2. messy _____

3. nighttime _____

4. upset _____

5. old _____

6. clean _____

7. cloudy _____

SYNONYMS

Synonyms are words that mean almost the same thing. Match the word on the left with its synonym on the right.

1. difficult   loud

2. thick   quiet

3. silent   hard

4. smile   dense

5. angry   smart

6. intelligent   grin

7. fast   mad

8. noisy   quick

THE POWER OF PREFIXES

A **prefix** is a letter or group of letters that go in front of a word and change the meaning of the word. Use the word box of prefixes to complete each word. There may be more than one answer for some words.

re-	un-	dis-

1. _____like

2. _____helpful

3. _____read

4. _____do

5. _____vise

6. _____appear

SUPER SUFFIXES

A **suffix** is a letter or collection of letters that go at the end of a word and change the meaning of the word. Use the word box of suffixes to complete each word.

-ness	-or	-hood

1. dark_____

2. child_____

3. act_____

4. mother_____

5. process_____

6. stubborn_____

IDIOMS

An **idiom** is a word or phrase that means something different than its literal meaning, such as "It's raining cats and dogs." For each idiom below, circle the answer that best fits its meaning.

Example: **It's <u>raining cats and dogs</u> in the overworld.**

    a. Cats and dogs are falling from the sky.

    b. It's cold outside.   (**c.**)It's raining hard.

1. **<u>Hit the books</u> now so you can play Minecraft later.**

    a. Study hard   **b.** Punch your books   **c.** Stay up late

2. **Destroying those skeletons was <u>a piece of cake</u>.**

    a. It was hard   **b.** It was sweet   **c.** It was easy

3. **He was <u>bent out of shape</u> because the griefer stole his loot.**

    a. Happy   **b.** Upset   **c.** Twisted in a pretzel

4. **The villagers fell in love and <u>tied the knot</u>.**

    a. They got divorced   **b.** They tied a rope in a knot

    c. They got married

5. **Alex has a <u>green thumb</u> in the garden.**

    a. She hates gardening   **b.** She is good at gardening

    c. Her thumb turns green when she gardens

6. **It was funny to watch the zombie dance because he had <u>two left feet</u>.**

    a. He was clumsy   **b.** He was a good dancer

    c. He was born with two left feet

DESCRIBING VERBS

Your writing will be more interesting if you use descriptive verbs. Compare these two sentences:

"Get out of here!" he said.

*"Get out of here!" he **hollered**.*

For each underlined word, write a word from the word box that better describes the action.

soared	staggered	clattered
cackled	sprinted	sparked

1. The minecart <u>went</u> through the mine.

   _____

2. The zombie <u>walked</u> through the village.

   _____

3. The witch <u>laughed</u> as she chased Alex away.

   _____

4. They <u>ran</u> away from the ghast's fireballs.

   _____

5. The Ender dragon <u>flew</u> through the sky.

   _____

6. The flint and steel <u>started</u> a fire.

   _____

INTERESTING ADJECTIVES

Choose your adjectives carefully. Pick the most interesting one you can think of. Compare these two sentences:

The potion was red.

*The potion was **scarlet**.*

For each underlined word, write two more adjectives that better describe the thing.

1. The zombie's clothes are <u>dirty</u>.

   _____   _____

2. The shulker makes <u>scary</u> noises.

   _____   _____

3. The Enderman is <u>tall</u>.

   _____   _____

4. The Ender dragon is <u>big</u>.

   _____   _____

5. Steve's farm has <u>pretty</u> flowers.

   _____   _____

6. Alex told a <u>funny</u> joke.

   _____   _____

ADD AN ADVERB

Your writing will be more interesting if you add an adverb to describe an action. Compare these two sentences:

"I won the game," she shouted.

*"I won the game," she shouted **happily**.*

For each underlined verb, add an adverb from the word box.

lovingly	**quickly**	**threateningly**
noisily	**carefully**	**jealously**

1. The husk <u>stared</u> _____ at the villagers.

2. Steve _____ <u>patted</u> his dog.

3. Alex saw the zombie coming toward her

   and _____ <u>took out</u> her sword.

4. The players <u>moved</u> _____ along the edge of the lava pit.

5. The piglin <u>grunted</u> _____ when it saw the player's shiny gold armor.

6. The ghast <u>screeched</u> _____ when it saw the players nearby.

LANGUAGE ARTS WORD SCRAMBLE

Unscramble the language arts words below. Use the words in the word box to help you.

adjective	conclusion	introduction
metaphor	prefix	simile	suffix

1. rxefip _____

2. vetdcjaei _____

3. limsei _____

4. sncuonlcoi _____

5. fxisfu _____

6. ruotnoictidn _____

7. rameptho _____

THE PROGRESSIVE TENSE

The **progressive tense** shows an action that is continuing or in progress. Fill out the chart below with the correct forms of the progressive tense. The first one is done for you.

PAST PROGRESSIVE	PRESENT PROGRESSIVE	FUTURE PROGRESSIVE
They were digging	They are digging	They will be digging
	I am gaming	
He was attacking		
		They will be mining
	She is battling	
They were playing		
		You will be farming
I was spawning		
	They are looting	

SOCIAL STUDIES WORD SCRAMBLE

Unscramble the social studies words below. Use the words in the word box to help you.

culture	colony	democracy
nation	rights	territory	vote

1. ncooly _____

2. taonin _____

3. ocdyaemcr _____

4. gsriht _____

5. etvo _____

6. ryrrettio _____

7. urtcleu _____

MATH WORDS SCRAMBLE

Unscramble the math words below. Use the words in the word box to help you.

measure	shape	divide
multiply	average	product	total

1. psaeh _____

2. emresua _____

3. latto _____

4. gevaare _____

5. iviedd _____

6. ypillmut _____

7. doptruc _____

IRREGULAR VERB TENSES

A **tense** tells the time when something happened. Fill in the chart with the correct tense of these irregular verbs. The first one is done for you.

BASE FORM	PAST	PRESENT	FUTURE
catch	caught	catches	will catch
teach		teaches	
begin	began		
drive			will drive
wear		wears	
draw	drew		

ORDER OF ADJECTIVES

When there are several adjectives describing a noun, the adjectives appear in a certain order:

1. *Number (e.g., four)*
2. *Size (e.g., large)*
3. *Shape (e.g., round)*
4. *Color (e.g., red)*
5. *Material (e.g., iron)*

Incorrect: *There are green, big, four slimes near the swamp.*
Correct: *There are four big, green slimes near the swamp.*

Put the adjectives in each phrase in the correct order.

1. black, square portal

_____

2. orange, three cats

_____

3. blue, large, five lapis lazuli blocks

_____

4. tiny, two, green emeralds

_____

Write your own Minecraft description using at least two adjectives in the correct order.

_____

HOMOPHONES

Homophones are words that sound the same but are spelled differently and mean different things. The words in parentheses are often confused for each other. Write the correct word on the line to complete the sentence.

1. This is _____ cobblestone house.
   (our, are)

2. The _____ wears a hat.
   (which, witch)

3. Let's _____ new skins for Minecraft.
   (buy, by)

4. The _____ in the tundra is snowy.
   (whether, weather)

5. The skeleton is bigger _____ the ocelot.
   (than, then)

6. The _____ said we can start a Minecraft club.
   (principle, principal)

7. Being a teacher requires _____ .
   (patience, patients)

USE YOUR WORDS!

Write a short story about the picture. Use some of the new words you've learned so far.

above	below	in front of
behind	next to	beside near

_____

_____

_____

_____

_____

SOCIAL STUDIES WORD SCRAMBLE

Unscramble the social studies words below. Use the words in the word box to help you.

> **boycott** **economy** **continent**
> **discovery** **citizen** **history** **terrain**

1. ytotboc _____

2. irtarne _____

3. zitecni _____

4. ncottnein _____

5. ysrohti _____

6. noycoem _____

7. rvedysico _____

THE POWER OF PREFIXES

A **prefix** is a letter or group of letters that go in front of a word and change the meaning of the word. Use the word box of prefixes to complete each word.

non-	co-	in-

1. _____sense

2. _____exist

3. _____visible

4. _____fiction

5. _____complete

6. _____author

SUPER SUFFIXES

A **suffix** is a letter or collection of letters that go at the
end of a word and change the meaning of the word. Use
the word box of suffixes to complete each word.

-ship	-able	-ish

1. friend_____

2. do_____

3. baby_____

4. leader_____

5. fool_____

6. suit_____

ROOT WORDS

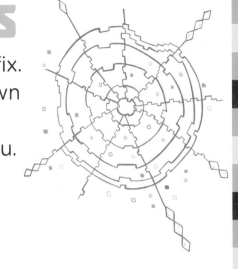

A **root word** does not have a prefix or a suffix. It is the basic part of a word and has its own meaning. Underline the root word in the examples below. The first one is done for you.

1. <u>sad</u>ness

2. unhappy

3. colorful

4. discomfort

5. artist

6. allowable

7. relearn

8. teacher

9. paperless

10. measurement

11. watchful

12. childlike

PROVERBS

A **proverb** is a short saying that gives advice or makes an observation about life.

Example:

> *An apple a day keeps the doctor away.*

For each proverb below, circle the answer that best fits its meaning.

1. **The early bird gets the worm.**
   a. Birds eat worms.
   b. You have to get up early if you want to succeed.
   c. Birds usually sleep late.

2. **Actions speak louder than words.**
   a. What you do is more important than what you say.
   b. Actors get the best speaking roles.
   c. Your actions can speak.

3. **Always put your best foot forward.**
   a. Your best foot is the one you kick a ball with.
   b. Walk with your right foot in front.
   c. Be the best version of yourself.

4. **All that glitters is not gold.**
   a. Not everything that looks attractive is actually valuable.
   b. Gold is glittery.
   c. Gold isn't worth much.

SIGHT WORD CROSSWORD

Sight words are words that appear many times in the books you read. Learn them and reading will be easier! Read the clues and write the sight word in the puzzle.

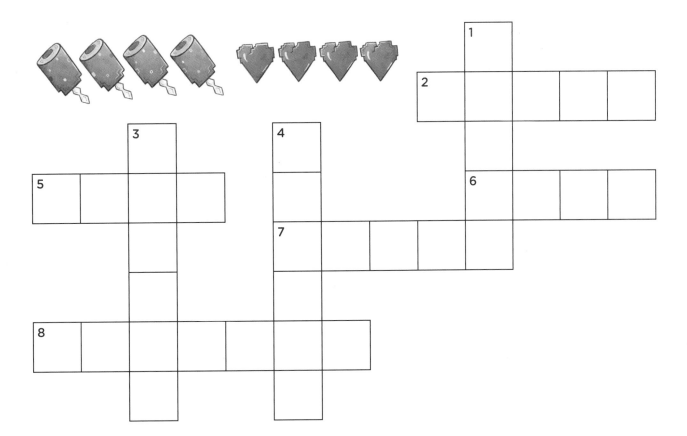

ACROSS

2 *a, e, i, o, or u*

5 Where food is grown

6 Something you sail on

7 Where a rocket ship goes

8 100 = one _____

DOWN

1 An animal that you ride

3 Someone you like to play with

4 What you do with your ears

PLURAL NOUNS WITH -Y

When a noun ends in **-y**, change the **-y** to **-ies** to make it plural. The first one is done for you.

SINGULAR	PLURAL
sky	skies
library	
poppy	
baby	
memory	
bunny	
pony	
enemy	

HOMONYMS

Homonyms are words that are spelled the same but have different meanings. Each homonym below has at least two meanings. Write two sentences with two different meanings of the same word. The first one is done for you.

1. rose

   The mob drop was a wither rose.

   I rose out of bed after respawning.

2. close

   _____

   _____

3. band

   _____

   _____

4. watch

   _____

   _____

5. tire

   _____

   _____

ANSWER KEY

PAGE 2

small	tiny	microscopic
good	great	excellent
worried	afraid	terrified
bad	awful	horrendous
walk	jog	run

POSSIBLE ANSWER: Steve is hiding behind a tree because he is **afraid** of the zombie.

PAGE 3

1. The location of the stronghold was **un**known.
2. Steve was **un**armed when he entered the Nether.
3. The potion of Invisibility made her **dis**appear.
4. The explosive green mob really **dis**likes cats.
5. I feel **un**safe when I see a piglin and I'm not wearing gold armor.
6. Milk can **un**do the effects of certain potions.

PAGE 4

1. The ghast screeches **loudly**.
2. Potion of Swiftness makes me move **quickly**.
3. The spotted spawn egg is **noticeably** different from the others.
4. She grew **increasingly** nervous as the zombies got closer.
5. The dolphins are **incredibly** skilled at finding treasure.
6. Without torches to help him, he fumbled **blindly** through the dark cave.

PAGE 5

POSSIBLE ANSWERS:

1. That little shulker is surprisingly **scary**.
2. Golden apples can be very **useful**.
3. It was a **clever** move to set that zombie trap.
4. It took me many **tries** to destroy the Ender dragon.
5. A diamond sword is extremely **durable**.

POSSIBLE ANSWERS:
happy, excited, thrilled

PAGE 6

1. **Whose** swamp hut is that?
2. **Which** of your swords will you use?
3. **Who** gave you that rabbit's foot?
4. **Who** is guarding the village?
5. **Whose** house do you want to meet at?

POSSIBLE ANSWERS:
Which potion will help me run faster?
The potion of Swiftness will help you run faster.

PAGE 7

PAGE 8

1. area
2. perimeter
3. unit
4. polygon
5. plot
6. equivalent
7. factor
8. multiple
9. quotient

PAGE 9

1. <u>Steve</u> caught a very large <u>fish</u>.
2. Steve was (excited) when he saw the (red) fish on his line.
3. Steve pulled on the rod and reeled in the fish.
4. The fish flapped noisily as Steve pulled ✓ quickly on the rod.

POSSIBLE ANSWERS:

5. **The frightened fish squirmed strongly on the line.**
6. **Steve was happy he had finally caught a fish.**

PAGE 10

1. tooth
2. woman
3. fish
4. person
5. foot
6. child
7. mouse
8. shelf

women
shelves
children
mice
teeth
fishes
people
feet

PAGE 11

SINGULAR	PLURAL
box	boxes
computer	computers
glass	glasses
book	books
class	classes
potato	potatoes
school	schools

PAGE 12

BASE FORM	PAST	PRESENT	FUTURE
play	played	plays	will play
call	called	calls	will call
walk	walked	walks	will walk
clean	cleaned	cleans	will clean
climb	climbed	climbs	will climb
look	looked	looks	will look

PAGE 13

1. Alex **ate** dinner.
2. Steve **slept** late.
3. He **went** to school yesterday.
4. She **flew** on the plane to see her grandma.
5. The teacher **spoke** to the class.
6. The ghast **stood** up tall.
7. I **wrote** an essay on my summer vacation.
8. She **read** the book for homework.

PAGE 14

ADJECTIVE	COMPARATIVE	SUPERLATIVE
tall	taller	tallest
loud	louder	loudest
good	better	best
smart	smarter	smartest
cold	colder	coldest
bright	brighter	brightest
soft	softer	softest
sweet	sweeter	sweetest

PAGE 15

1. The sun is **brighter** in the summer than in the winter.
2. The Enderman is **taller** than the zombie.
3. Alex is the **smartest** person I know.
4. This pillow is the **softest** one.
5. Minecraft cookies are **sweeter** than mushroom stew.
6. The Snowy Tundra is the **coldest** biome I've visited.
7. This Minecraft update is **better** than the last one.
8. The wither's cry was the **loudest** thing I have ever heard.

PAGE 16

1. opinion
2. adverb
3. character
4. fact
5. conflict
6. phrase
7. dialogue

PAGE 17

1. herbivore
2. prey
3. erosion
4. carnivore
5. microscope
6. community
7. volcano

PAGE 18

1. The witch's potion
2. The horse's saddle
3. The zombie's arm
4. Alex's sword
5. The chicken's egg
6. The player's minecart
7. Steve's pickaxe

PAGE 19

SINGULAR NOUN	PLURAL NOUN	PLURAL POSSESSIVE NOUN
ghast	ghasts	ghasts'
player	players	players'
zombie	zombies	zombies'
creeper	creepers	creepers'
dragon	dragons	dragons'
villager	villagers	villagers'
librarian	librarians	librarians'
witch	witches	witches'
griefer	griefers	griefers'

PAGE 20

PAGE 21

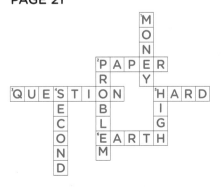

PAGE 22

1. fearful
2. helpless
3. colorful
4. speechless
5. hopeful
6. endless

POSSIBLE ANSWERS:

It was thoughtless of Steve to leave Alex to fight alone.

The quiet of the forest biome felt peaceful.

PAGE 23

1. quiet
2. above
3. empty
4. cold
5. small
6. enemy
7. awake

below
friend
large
loud
full
asleep
hot

POSSIBLE ANSWERS:

happy, excited, joyful

PAGE 24

PAGE 25

BASE FORM	PAST TENSE
eat	ate
think	thought
throw	threw
sing	sang
hear	heard
go	went
is	was
sit	sat

PAGE 26

1. families
2. flies
3. berries
4. babies
5. cities
6. countries
7. memories

PAGE 27

1. next to
2. inside
3. beneath
4. in front of
5. behind
6. above
7. below

PAGE 28

5 Finally, Steve shut the cage with the bunny inside.
3 Then, Steve placed a line of carrots leading to the cage.
1 First, Steve collected a bunch of carrots.
2 Next, Steve placed a cage on the ground.
4 Eventually, the bunny wandered into the cage.

PAGE 29

1. there
2. two
3. It's
4. hear
5. You're
6. piece

PAGE 30

1. The witch's hut
2. The spiders' cave
3. The dragon's eyes
4. Alex's torches
5. The player's level
6. The ocelot's fish
7. Steve's crafting table

PAGE 31

PAGE 32

PAGE 33
1. volume
2. habitat
3. matter
4. ecosystem
5. solid
6. predator
7. gravity
8. energy

PAGE 34
1. hard
2. neat
3. daytime
4. happy
5. young
6. dirty
7. sunny

PAGE 35
1. difficult — hard
2. thick — dense
3. silent — loud
4. smile — grin
5. angry — mad
6. intelligent — smart
7. fast — quick
8. noisy — quiet

PAGE 36
1. dislike (or unlike)
2. unhelpful
3. reread (or unread)
4. undo (or redo)
5. revise
6. disappear (or reappear)

PAGE 37
1. darkness
2. childhood
3. actor
4. motherhood
5. processor
6. stubbornness

PAGE 38
1. a
2. c
3. b
4. c
5. b
6. a

PAGE 39
1. clattered
2. staggered
3. cackled
4. sprinted
5. soared
6. sparked

PAGE 40
POSSIBLE ANSWERS:
1. filthy, tattered
2. terrifying, frightful
3. towering, giant
4. huge, enormous
5. gorgeous, beautiful
6. hilarious, side-splitting

PAGE 41
1. threateningly
2. lovingly
3. quickly
4. carefully
5. quietly
6. noisily

PAGE 42
1. prefix
2. adjective
3. simile
4. conclusion
5. suffix
6. introduction
7. metaphor

PAGE 43

PAST PROGRESSIVE	PRESENT PROGRESSIVE	FUTURE PROGRESSIVE
They were digging	They are digging	They will be digging
I was gaming	I am gaming	I will be gaming
He was attacking	He is attacking	He will be attacking
They were mining	They are mining	They will be mining
She was battling	She is battling	She will be battling
They were playing	They are playing	They will be playing
You were farming	You are farming	You will be farming
I was spawning	I am spawning	I will be spawning
They were looting	They are looting	They will be looting

PAGE 44
1. colony
2. nation
3. democracy
4. rights
5. vote
6. territory
7. culture

PAGE 45
1. shape
2. measure
3. total
4. average
5. divide
6. multiply
7. product

PAGE 46

BASE FORM	PAST	PRESENT	FUTURE
catch	caught	catches	will catch
teach	taught	teaches	will teach
begin	began	begins	will begin
drive	drove	drives	will drive
wear	wore	wears	will wear
draw	drew	draws	will draw

PAGE 47
1. square, black portal
2. three orange cats
3. five large, blue, lapis lazuli blocks
4. two tiny, green emeralds
Answers will vary but should follow the correct order.

PAGE 48
1. our
2. witch
3. buy
4. weather
5. than
6. principal
7. patience

PAGE 49
Answers will vary.

PAGE 50
1. boycott
2. terrain
3. citizen
4. continent
5. history
6. economy
7. discovery

PAGE 51
1. nonsense
2. coexist
3. invisible
4. nonfiction
5. incomplete
6. coauthor

PAGE 52
1. friendship
2. doable
3. babyish
4. leadership
5. foolish
6. suitable

PAGE 53
1. sadness
2. unhappy
3. colorful
4. discomfort
5. artist
6. allowable
7. relearn
8. teacher
9. paperless
10. measurement
11. watchful
12. childlike

PAGE 54
1. b
2. a
3. c
4. a

PAGE 55

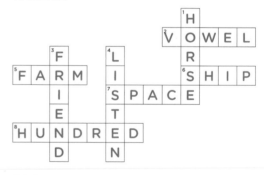

PAGE 56

SINGULAR	PLURAL
sky	skies
library	libraries
poppy	poppies
baby	babies
memory	memories
bunny	bunnies
pony	ponies
enemy	enemies

PAGE 57
Answers will vary but should show two different meanings for each word.